"Blossom in Faith
Change. Grow. Emerge."

by

Wendy Davis

Dedication

This guided journal is dedicated to all the women in my life who have special places in my heart.

To my mother, Charla, and my two daughters, Kyra and Amirah, I love you dearly!

Note from the Author

I am the one to know firsthand how it feels to walk in fear, timidity, and insecurity. Those negative attributes controlled my life in some form or another. But, I still pressed my way. I have had to overcome quite a few feats (such as nursing school, starting a business, and teaching women's Sunday school classes, to name a few) while doing so with fear and nervousness. However, with God, I did those things! I held on to what HE told me!

It is true; sometimes, I felt confident, and some days I struggled. Yes, I know it is easier for some women to walk in boldness and confidence, yet, others struggle daily. For some, confidence comes naturally, while it is a growing process for others. For those who are trying to find that confidence, whatever you do, you must not let fear, timidity, or insecurity hold you back from what God has called you. I believe you have gifts, skills, and talents to share, but fear and doubt are holding you back. It is time for a mindset shift. You are among the many voices who need to speak up for the weak, the forgotten, and the oppressed. Holy Spirit-led, your words, and deeds are the tools to help set others free.

I hope you take some time and go through this journal to learn the truths of God's Word. He wants you to thrive in every area of your life. And I want you to grow, change, and emerge from the fearful and insecure woman to the woman whose voice, skills, gifts, and talents will change her environment, community, and the world.

As my doctor recently told me, I am now telling you, "The world is waiting on you!"

Wendy

Table of Contents

Note from the Author..iii

About this Journal..v

Sections

      Mindset..2

      Courage...21

      Grow..40

      Overcome...59

      Emerge...78

Purpose and Vision..96

Prayers 99

Closing remarks from the Author...120

About this Journal

This faith-based journal features inspiring quotes and Scriptures and intriguing questions and prompts. The five sections include Mindset, Courage, Grow, Overcome, and Emerge. These five areas help strengthen and build your courage as you grow in Christ.

Each section has seven focus scriptures, four guided prompts (per each scripture) to answer, and an extra page for your notes or prayers. Also included are inspirational quotes and guided prompts throughout the journal, with additional pages for your personal vision and prayers (at the end).

It is suggested to study and meditate (Psalms 119:15) on one focused scripture per week. However, you can go through this journal at your own pace.

Journal daily or take your time to reflect and apply His Word to help shift your mindset. Jesus wants you to flourish and thrive no matter what you have been through and are currently facing. Because, like a butterfly, you are meant to change, grow, and emerge.

Take a moment to write something POSITIVE or what you LOVE most about yourself.

If you have moments of doubt or fear, come back and read this page aloud.

MINDSET

God wants you to change how you see yourself. You are someone exceptional. You are fearfully and wonderfully made.

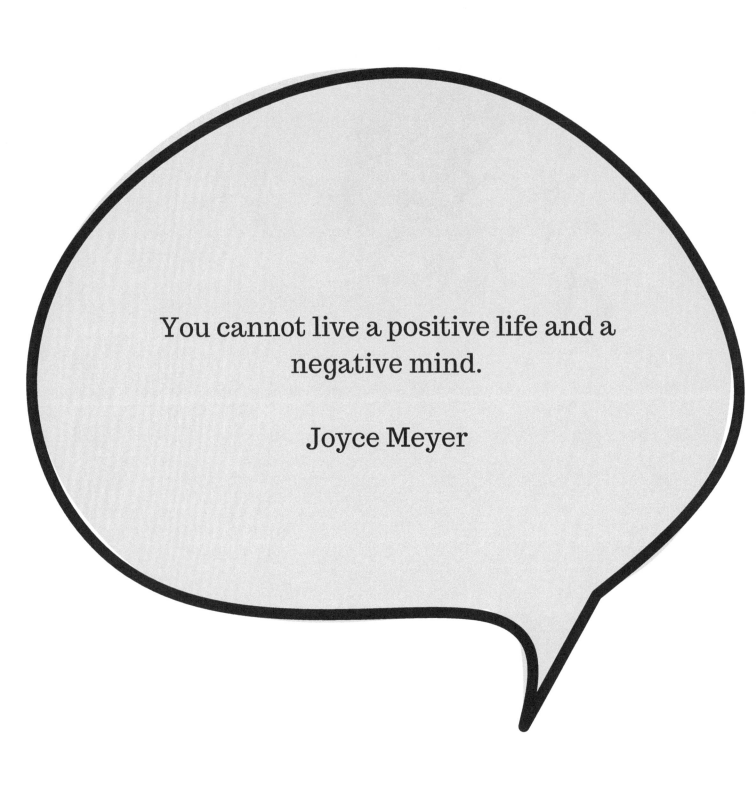

You cannot live a positive life and a negative mind.

Joyce Meyer

Your mindset can determine your answers to problems, the altitude of your success, your attitude towards others, and your actions in life situations. If you have a fearful mindset, fear will dominate. If you have a negative mindset, pessimistic or harmful reactions will likely follow. But, if you change your perspective and allow the goodness of God to flow and guide your thoughts and ways, how much better would life be?

Coach Wen

Do you have a fixed or negative mindset or a growth mindset? What will you do to improve your growth mindset?

_____

_____

_____

_____

_____

_____

_____

_____

_____

MINDSET

Date :

Focus: Renewed

Scripture: Ephesians 4: 22-24

What word or phrase speaks most to your heart?

How does this scripture directly relate to your life right now?

What could you do differently to align yourself with this scripture?

Your own additional prayer, thoughts, reflections, or actions:

NOTES

MINDSET

Date :

Focus: Forget the Past

Scripture: Philippians 3: 13-14

What word or phrase speaks most to your heart?

How does this scripture directly relate to your life right now?

What could you do differently to align yourself with this scripture?

Your additional prayer, thoughts, reflections, or actions:

NOTES

MINDSET

Date :

Focus: Spiritually Minded

Scripture: Romans 8: 5-9

What word or phrase speaks most to your heart?

How does this scripture directly relate to your life right now?

What could you do differently to align yourself with this scripture?

Your additional prayers, thoughts, reflections, or actions:

NOTES

MINDSET

Date :

Focus: Sober-minded

Scripture: 1 Peter 1: 13-15

What word or phrase speaks
most to your heart?

How does this scripture directly
relate to your life right now?

What could you do differently to align yourself with this
scripture?

Your additional prayer, thoughts, reflections, or actions:

NOTES

MINDSET

Date :

Focus: Wavering Mind

Scripture: James 1: 5-8

What word or phrase speaks most to your heart?

How does this scripture directly relate to your life right now?

What could you do differently to align yourself with this scripture?

Your additional prayer, thoughts, reflections, or actions:

NOTES

MINDSET

Date :

Focus: Thought life

Scripture: Philippians 4: 8-9

What word or phrase speaks
most to your heart?

How does this scripture directly
relate to your life right now?

What could you do differently to align yourself with this
scripture?

Your additional prayer, thoughts, reflections, or actions:

NOTES

MINDSET

Focus: Transformed Mind

Scripture: Romans 12: 1-2

What word of phrase speaks
most to your heart?

How does this scripture directly
relate to your life right now?

What could you do differently to align yourself with this
scripture?

Your additional prayer, thoughts, reflections, or actions:

18

NOTES

Use Scripture to help control your thoughts the way God encourages you to.

What motivates you to study more about God's Word?

_____

_____

_____

_____

_____

_____

_____

_____

_____

_____

COURAGE

Do not fear! Jesus is
with you!

_____

We may feel fear, but we do not have to give in to it. We can do whatever we need and want to, even if we have to "do it afraid." Courage is not the absence of fear; it is action in the presence of fear.

Joyce Meyer

Remember the Bible story of David and Goliath and how the Lord helped David defeat the giant? The story says David ran towards Goliath. That was some courage! David went forward in the strength of the Lord.

When obstacles come your way, pray for discernment, know the Lord is with you, and do not shrink back in fear. Change your mindset and understand that in Jesus, you have the strength it takes to move forward amid the battle. You may be quiet or reserved but do not have to operate from a place of fear. You, too, can face the giants in your life with the Lord on your side. Go forward. Be confident and courageous!

Coach Wen

Even if you don't think so, you are courageous. Think back to a time when you stood up in the face of adversity.

How did that look and feel?

_____

_____

_____

_____

_____

_____

_____

_____

_____

_____

COURAGE

Date :

Focus: Be Courageous

Scripture: Joshua 1:9

What word or phrase speaks
most to your heart?

How does this scripture directly
relate to your life right now?

What could you do differently to align yourself with this
scripture?

Your additional prayer, thoughts, reflections, or actions:

NOTES

COURAGE

Date :

Focus: No Fear

Scripture: Deuteronomy 20:34

What word or phrase speaks most to your heart?

How does this scripture directly relate to your life right now?

What could you do differently to align yourself with this scripture?

Your additional prayer, thoughts, reflections, or actions:

NOTES

COURAGE

Date :

Focus: No Shame

Scripture: 2 Timothy 1: 7-8

What word or phrase speaks
most to your heart?

How does this scripture directly
relate to your life right now?

What could you do differently to align yourself with this
scripture?

Your additional prayer, thoughts, reflections, or actions:

NOTES

COURAGE

Date :

Focus: Strength and Help

Scripture: Isaiah 41:10

What word or phrase speaks
most to your heart?

How does this scripture directly
relate to your life right now?

What could you do differently to align yourself with this
scripture?

Your additional prayer, thoughts, reflections, or actions:

NOTES

COURAGE

Date :

Focus: All Things

Scripture: Philippians 4:13

What word or phrase speaks
most to your heart?

How does this scripture directly
relate to your life right now?

What could you do differently to align yourself with this
scripture?

Your additional prayer, thoughts, reflections, or actions:

NOTES

COURAGE

Date :

Focus: Eagles

Scripture: Isaiah 40: 29-31

What word or phrase speaks most to your heart?

How does this scripture directly relate to your life right now?

What could you do differently to align yourself with this scripture?

Your additional prayer, thoughts, reflections, or actions:

NOTES

COURAGE

Date :

Focus: Confidence

Scripture: Psalms 27: 1-3

What word or phrase speaks most to your heart?

How does this scripture directly relate to your life right now?

What could you do differently to align yourself with this scripture?

Your additional prayer, thoughts, reflections, or actions:

NOTES

Name five people you think are courageous. What makes them brave? Can you draw from their strength?

God places people in your life to help you.

GROW

Bloom and grow
where you are
planted.

Courage is not defined by those who fought
and did not fall but by those who fought, fell,
and rose again.
~~~Anonymous~~~

Let us talk about the task of gardening. It is work, no doubt! If you are an avid gardener, you are aware of how gardening works. You prepare the ground---plant the seed---water when necessary---and let nature take its course.

Well, in your life, you must put in work too! "How so?" you may ask. As a Christian believer, you are responsible for seeking, praying, and studying to develop your walk in Christ.

You cannot remain the same. You must keep moving forward! You need to do your part (plant), then someone (a friend, minister, coach) comes along to help you (water), and God will then give the increase (growth). You are meant to move forward and make progress!

Coach Wen

Often, change can help you to grow. What changes have you noticed coming your way? Are you resisting or welcoming those changes, and why?

_____

_____

_____

_____

_____

_____

_____

_____

_____

_____

GROW

Focus: Fullness of Christ

Scripture: Ephesians 4: 13-16

What word or phrase speaks most to your heart?

How does this scripture directly relate to your life right now?

What could you do differently to align yourself with this scripture?

Your additional prayer, thoughts, reflections, or actions:

NOTES

GROW

Focus: Be an Example

Scripture: I Timothy 4: 12-15

What word or phrase speaks most to your heart?

How does this scripture directly relate to your life right now?

What could you do differently to align yourself with this scripture?

Your additional prayer, thoughts, reflections, or actions:

NOTES

GROW

Date :

Focus: Lay Aside Evil

Scripture: 1 Peter 2: 1-2

What word or phrase speaks most to your heart?

How does this scripture directly relate to your life right now?

What could you do differently to align yourself with this scripture?

Your additional prayer, thoughts, reflections, or actions:

NOTES

GROW

Date :

Focus: Increase in Knowledge

Scripture: Colossians 1: 9-10

What word or phrase speaks most to your heart?

How does this scripture directly relate to your life right now?

What could you do differently to align yourself with this scripture?

Your additional prayer, thoughts, reflections, or actions:

NOTES

GROW

Date :

Focus: Become an Adult

Scripture: 1 Corinthians 13: 11

What word or phrase speaks
most to your heart?

How does this scripture directly
relate to your life right now?

What could you do differently to align yourself with this
scripture?

Your additional prayer, thoughts, reflections, or
actions:

NOTES

GROW

Date :

Focus: Be Established

Scripture: Colossians 2: 6-8

What word or phrase speaks
most to your heart?

How does this scripture directly
relate to your life right now?

What could you do differently to align yourself with this
scripture?

Your additional prayer, thoughts, reflections, or
actions:

NOTES

GROW

Date :

Focus: Stay in the Word

Scripture: Joshua 1:8

What word or phrase speaks most to your heart?

How does this scripture directly relate to your life right now?

What could you do differently to align yourself with this scripture?

Your additional prayer, thoughts, reflections, or actions:

NOTES

Sometimes things do not go as you plan. Describe a moment where you felt disappointed or experienced some lack of success.

What have you learned, or how have you grown from this?

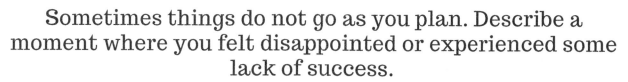

_____

_____

_____

_____

_____

_____

_____

_____

_____

OVERCOME

Say this out loud: This
too shall pass; I will
overcome this!

Living in freedom means learning how to walk again- learning how to walk God's way for a change- because listen, you can be 100 percent saved and still spend the majority of your time in Egypt. Unbelievers aren't the only ones who contribute to Egypt's overcrowding.

Priscilla Shirer

Do you know what it takes to overcome challenges? It takes belief in Jesus, a growth mindset, courage in adversity, possible support from others, and perseverance. Life can be complicated; that is for sure. But, if you stay on the right track to your destination, you will see victory.

Coach Wen

"You are an overcomer; stay in the fight until the final round"...Mandisa

What is the one thing you want to overcome right now? Then, take a moment to consider what you can do to overcome this.

_____

_____

_____

_____

_____

_____

_____

_____

_____

_____

OVERCOME

Focus: Victory

Scripture: 1 John 5: 4-5

What word or phrase speaks most to your heart?

How does this scripture directly relate to your life right now?

What could you do differently to align yourself with this scripture?

Your additional prayer, thoughts, reflections, or actions?

NOTES

OVERCOME

Focus: Nothing Shall Seperate Us

Scripture: Romans 8: 36-39

What word or phrase speaks most to your heart?

How does this scripture directly relate to your life right now?

What could you do differently to align yourself with this scripture?

Your additional prayer, thoughts, reflections, or actions?

65

NOTES

OVERCOME

Focus: He is Greater

Scripture: 1 John 4: 4

What word or phrase speaks
most to your heart?

How does this scripture directly
relate to your life right now?

What could you do differently to align yourself with this
scripture?

Your additional prayer, thoughts, reflections, or actions?

NOTES

OVERCOME

Focus: Working for You

Scripture: Romans 8: 28

What word or phrase speaks
most to your heart?

How does this scripture directly
relate to your life right now?

What could you do differently to align yourself with this
scripture?

Your additional prayer, thoughts, reflections, or actions?

69

NOTES

OVERCOME

Date :

Focus: He Hears

Scripture: Psalms 3: 3-5

What word or phrase speaks
most to your heart?

How does this scripture directly
relate to your life right now?

What could you do differently to align yourself with this
scripture?

Your additional prayer, thoughts, reflections, or actions?

NOTES

OVERCOME

Date :

Focus: Triumph

Scripture: 2 Corinthians 2: 14

What word or phrase speaks
most to your heart?

How does this scripture directly
relate to your life right now?

What could you do differently to align yourself with this
scripture?

Your additional prayer, thoughts, reflections, or actions?

NOTES

OVERCOME

Focus: Do Not Tremble

Scripture: Deuteronomy 20: 1-4

What word or phrase speaks
most to your heart?

How does this scripture directly
relate to your life right now?

What could you do differently to align yourself with this
scripture?

Your additional prayer, thoughts, reflections, or actions?

NOTES

Read this Scripture
Isaiah 40:31

How does it speak to you?

77

EMERGE

God gives you the ability
to emerge victoriously.
Be FREE!

We delight in the beauty of the butterfly but rarely admit the changes
it has gone through to achieve that beauty.

Maya Angelou

You may be going through one of the toughest seasons of your life. You may need to fight, cry, scream, pray, and do whatever else to make it through. Often, those rough times are meant to make you stronger.

And while in this season of pressing and stretching, keep your head up and your eyes focused on HIM.

Keep the faith. Stay the course.

May the victory forever be your portion!

List three obstacles that may lie in your way of becoming your best self.

Then list two solutions that could help you emerge from those obstacles.

_____

_____

_____

_____

_____

_____

_____

_____

_____

_____

EMERGE

Focus: Liberty

Scripture: 2 Corinthians 3: 17

What word or phrase speaks
most to your heart?

How does this scripture directly
relate to your life right now?

What could you do differently to align yourself with
this scripture?

Your additional prayer, thoughts, reflections, or
actions?

NOTES

EMERGE

Date :

Focus: Free Indeed

Scripture: John 8: 36

What word or phrase speaks most to your heart?

How does this scripture directly relate to your life right now?

What could you do differently to align yourself with this scripture?

Your additional prayer, thoughts, reflections, or actions?

NOTES

EMERGE

Focus: Don't Go Back

Scripture: Galatians 5: 1

What word or phrase speaks
most to your heart?

How does this scripture directly
relate to your life right now?

What could you do differently to align yourself with
this scripture?

Your additional prayer, thoughts, reflections, or
actions?

NOTES

EMERGE

Focus: Speak Out

Scripture: Luke 4: 18

What word or phrase speaks most to your heart?

How does this scripture directly relate to your life right now?

What could you do differently to align yourself with this scripture?

Your additional prayer, thoughts, reflections, or actions?

NOTES

EMERGE

Date :

Focus: Called Out

Scripture: 1 Peter 2: 9

What word or phrase speaks most to your heart?

How does this scripture directly relate to your life right now?

What could you do differently to align yourself with this scripture?

Your additional prayer, thoughts, reflections, or actions?

NOTES

EMERGE

Focus: Boldness in Christ

Scripture: Ephesians 3: 11-12

What word or phrase speaks most to your heart?

How does this scripture directly relate to your life right now?

What could you do differently to align yourself with this scripture?

Your additional prayer, thoughts, reflections, or actions?

NOTES

EMERGE

Date :

Focus: Come Forth

Scripture: John 11: 43-44

What word or phrase speaks most to your heart?

How does this scripture directly relate to your life right now?

What could you do differently to align yourself with this scripture?

Your additional prayer, thoughts, reflections, or actions?

NOTES

What do you believe is your unique purpose?

After going through this journal, what do you expect of yourself moving forward?

Now, take the time to write your vision statement.
Write it. Read it. Run with it...(Habakkuk 2:2)

PRAYERS

(YOU CAN MOST CERTAINLY USE THE
NEXT PAGES TO WRITE OUT YOUR
PRAYER REQUESTS, ANSWERED
PRAYERS, WORDS OF CONFIRMATION,
OR WHATEVER YOU WANT.)

PRAYERS

_____

_____

_____

_____

_____

_____

_____

_____

_____

_____

PRAYERS

_____

_____

_____

_____

_____

_____

_____

_____

_____

_____

PRAYERS

_____

_____

_____

_____

_____

_____

_____

_____

_____

_____

PRAYERS

_____

_____

_____

_____

_____

_____

_____

_____

_____

_____

PRAYERS

_____

_____

_____

_____

_____

_____

_____

_____

_____

_____

_____

PRAYERS

_____

_____

_____

_____

_____

_____

_____

_____

_____

_____

PRAYERS

_____

_____

_____

_____

_____

_____

_____

_____

_____

_____

_____

PRAYERS

_____

_____

_____

_____

_____

_____

_____

_____

_____

_____

PRAYERS

_____

_____

_____

_____

_____

_____

_____

_____

_____

_____

_____

PRAYERS

_____

_____

_____

_____

_____

_____

_____

_____

_____

_____

PRAYERS

PRAYERS

PRAYERS

_____

_____

_____

_____

_____

_____

_____

_____

_____

_____

_____

PRAYERS

_____

_____

_____

_____

_____

_____

_____

_____

_____

_____

PRAYERS

_____

_____

_____

_____

_____

_____

_____

_____

_____

_____

PRAYERS

_____

_____

_____

_____

_____

_____

_____

_____

_____

_____

PRAYERS

_____

_____

_____

_____

_____

_____

_____

_____

_____

_____

_____

PRAYERS

PRAYERS

PRAYERS

Do not let anyone make you deny what is in you! You are precious and valuable in the Father's eye!

Coach Wen

Made in the USA
Monee, IL
15 September 2023

42629921R00070